new words {press}
New York, NY
www.newwordspress.com

new words {press} is a sponsored non-profit poetry press dedicated to elevating emerging and established trans* and gender-expansive poetic voices, building community, and sharing knowledge.

ISBN: 978-1-968528-01-0

Cover art by Aggie Johnson
Cover layout by brooklyn baggett
Typesetting by brooklyn baggett
Font: Bakersville, EB Garamond, and Lora

Printed in the United States of America

MYTHWEAVER

poems

Birch Wiley

new words {press}

A TRANS* & GENDER-EXPANSIVE POETRY PRESS

I'm grateful to write in a time when a shared "canon" is less expected than it once was, when there is a wide landscape of traditions that writers create from. This is a much more interesting way to make literature, but it does make keeping all our source material straight a challenge.

To expect every reader to have even a glancing familiarity with the Greco-Roman myths referenced in this text, then, would be unreasonable. At the end of the book you'll find a Notes section where, in order of appearance, there is a brief description of each mythical allusion. There is also a bibliography that includes a list of the specific translations, interpretations, and non-fiction texts that I drew from while writing.

– Birch Wiley

7 MYTHWEAVER

CRETAN INTERLUDE

GLUKUS

THE CAENEID

Mythweaver

after 'Landscape with the Fall of Icarus' by Pieter Bruegel the Elder

Tell yourself a story
about yourself until
it is true. Now, try again.

Icarus forgives his father
as the wax falls off his wings.
Find a new answer

for that old question –
all problems can't be solved
with the tools that made them.

Where do we go for relief
when the reality
of our bodies fails us?

What to do when we want
to say what we mean
but we can't find language

that means what we need to say?
Go deeper into the words.
Pull truth out with your teeth –

from the cliff you can just see
white legs vanish into water.
Now, follow him down.

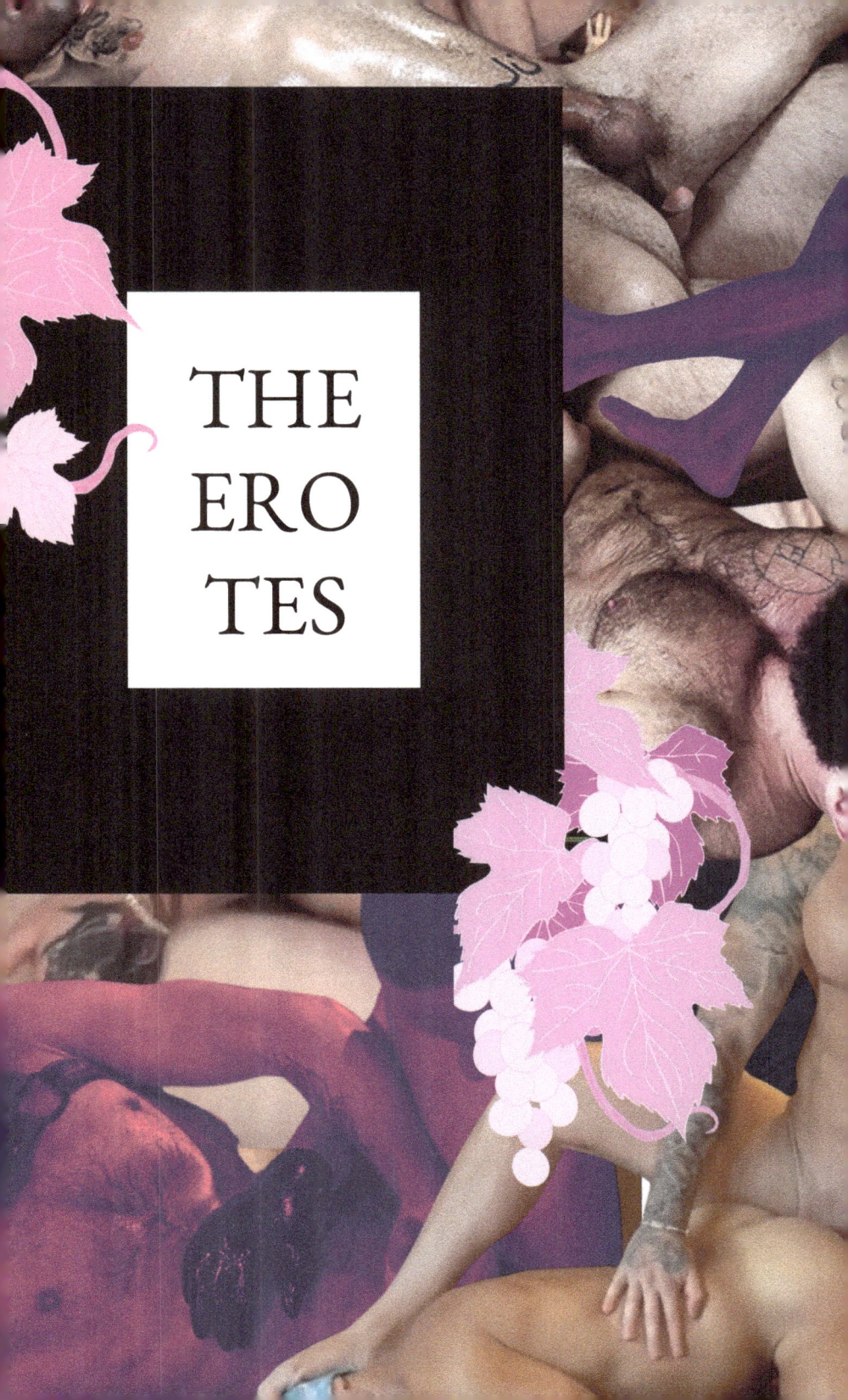

THE ERO TES

Eros

Worse than all the fevers failed
to break. Easy to shatter as milk
glass. Bloody as the fox hound's teeth.
Stings like a splinter, digs deeper
when you hunt after it with tweezers.
Harder to drive away than salesmen
peddling eternity on your doorstep –
feels like you'd be better off closing
the blinds, pretending not to be home –
but then there are early hours
in a strange bed. Watch the light
come down. It makes odd shapes of furniture
you thought you'd learned in the night. Beside you
someone sleeps. Try not to wake them.

Anteros

It's an old story, a boring story:
I loved someone, I left him anyway.
The train moved under me, and I knew
I was wrong. I gave some reason –
his unemployment, my drunkenness – but
truth is, I feared I was incapable
of being loved. The fear made itself true.
I haven't seen him since. Some nights, though,
his scent in my sheets – his laugh shaking out
of the curtains – his warmth in the close dark.
There is no moral, this is just another
story about learning how to live
with what we chose. Still – our foreheads pressed
together. The way our eyelashes touched.

Phthonus

o thick necked   thick veined   thick armed   thick skulled boy
young blunt bold   bucking over my body
and the sweat drips down his neck   drips off his eaves
and I savor his salt   mesmerized
by keen edges   muscled limbs move
in hypnotic rhythm   deep-belly grunts
split lips   my hands slide off his wax-smooth
chest   his eyes gone   someplace far inside
and where am I?   not inside myself   but
pressed against my own glass   imagine
how easy and dumb   to live in flesh
you don't have to think about   when he
comes and rolls off and starts to snore I watch
him   he sleeps the sleep   of animals

Hymen

God bless faggots in white top hats and tails,
soft butch dykes in paired ties, pumps dyed to match,
picket fence queers joining PTAs.
The aging Chamber of Commerce Chair
tied me to his marital bed
before he whipped me, called me by his husband's
name – now I'm nameless, just his good boy.
It might have been nice to have this life
fit clean and simple into tax forms,
to pay for my own TV subscriptions,
buy a golden doodle, join a country
club. Maybe it was spite that made me leave
my jockstrap in their blissful-wedded sheets.

◂

Himeros

We catch each other's orbit in the crowd –
a friend's birthday party and we've never
met – but I watch you out of the corner
of each eye, try to be subtle trailing
you from room to room, watch you fill your
cup, cackle at a joke I didn't hear,
flash teeth bright as wet pavement in sunlight,
and no one else here guesses what you are.
I know you the way I know a song.
We will take our time falling into bed
and I'm sure I'll be clumsy, shy, not quite
as debonair as I'd hoped – tonight though
we're tied by a tight cord of want that we fear,
but not quite enough to cut it – not yet.

Hermaphroditus

their cock turns cunt   all soft folds   pink clit head
in a bed of black fur   my tongue moves flat
against rocking hips   their fists tight above bound
wrists   my hands around thighs slick with sweat
we body dyke-fag pleasure   our skin wet
with each other's need   we forget ourselves
forget sidewalk slurs   long hours waiting
on clinic results   nights crying on trains
under rivers   talking down lovers   friends
all lost under pant   sweat   beg   beg to breed
these bodies   emptied of their potential
still scissor desperate   to make something new
with our big   outrageous   hungry   bodies
o   our sterile bodies   make miracles

Pothos

Miss you but won't call – so sure you don't
replay my tongue the way I replay
yours. All day it comes to me, our skin
on skin open mouthed nights, not fucking but
teasing pleasure out of hours half-clothed
in dreamless beds. All day your voice heavy
on the back of my neck, your whimper, sigh,
moan, invocation of god. We are not
in love yet, so scared of falling and not
catching the other's hand, but all day you
and your crooked-tooth smile, smudged glasses,
bray-bell laugh, restless bird fidget. Your heat
radiates while you sleep. A little sun –
necessary, beautiful, just out of reach.

Hedylogos

say baby   say lover   say darlin'
say sweetness   angel   faggot   honey   say
baby   baby   baby   call me peaches
and cream   buttercup   sunshine   sugar
good boy   good slut   best thing you never knew
to look for   don't love kitten   butterfly
boo   dumpling   doll face   more of a sweet prince
partner-in-crime   stud   even candy
if you look   hungry enough saying it
you don't call me anything   these days
I miss our   front   seat   heavy petting
all the pets   I got to be for you
I miss   the lengths you'd go to not to
call me some other   faggot   baby's   name

SAP
PHI
CS

The Other Sappho

I'm walking on neon Hudson shore when the truck
pulls up onto the sand, gravel, stones, driftwood.
Teal paint curls from rotted wheel wells, chrome
          shines through rust,

headlights salt-veiled. Behind the wheel my other
body rolls the window down with a blunt nub
of a finger   green water sheets down the door.
          He smiles through holes

in his cheeks   wet cigarette in his lips.
Got a light? Maypole forearms shed their muscle.
I put a Cheyenne in each mouth, light up, lean
          against the hood. We shoot

the shit   the engine idles   we talk about
this river's bottom   all the washing machines
and freak fish   my college degree he never
          finished   lovers who

ruined his life   lovers I don't remember.
I didn't drive off the Tappan Zee Bridge so
I figured I'm better now   at least better
          enough. Our laughter

shakes walnuts and acorns out of treetops.
Maybe I'll weight my pockets with sobriety
coins   follow behind   wade into the water
          trailing his exhaust.

Ganymede / Zeus

Behind us his bedroom buzzes neon purple
against black lacquer and acrylic   refracts
careful mirrors you live inside when you
         are in his bed.

Your collected reflections splatter the walls
this room heated all seasons   hot house tomato
ripening. He bends over the telescope
         on the balcony

trains its eye on a red moon over the skyline
lets me replace him there   watch her smile wan
over the hollow thrash of metal and glass.
         Dry hands slide into

my waistband. Always as if he must   distract?
seduce?   apologize?   As if envelopes
of cash against skin weren't proof enough this
         is a sure thing.

I can feel the envelope until   nothing
but wet air   denim on carpet   nothing
but lush light drowning the moon. He bucks, confused
         dog on his owner's

most provocative pillowcase. Telescope drifts
down into city windows   an elbow   there
eclipsed by cabinet corners   stirring? A man
         smiles   touches her

waist?   hip? Bends to kiss   cheek?   neck?   lips? Surfaces
open mouthed   laugh?   shout?   Before they can reveal
the shape of their night   the man here pulls me back
         to plastic   blacklight haze.

Labors of Heracles

"And all the wrong he did before, loose it."

  - Sappho, translated by Anne Carson

Told my mother it was the cat knocked over
the concrete bird bath she'd just watched me topple
through the kitchen window. Called a boy some name
        on the playground.

Slapped a girl across the face in middle school
I think underneath a Japanese maple
red light hanging over us. Cornered a girl
        in a high school stairwell,

tried to make her kiss me. Mocked someone in class
for pronouncing a word in accents I didn't
recognize. Knocked the closet door off its track with
        my body's high rage.

Broke the garage window stacking firewood.
Fucked that woman in that hotel room, our friend
asleep in the next bed. Fucked a friend's ex, too.
        Turned from a lover

when they turned my hand away, our bodies curled
spine to spine, sleepless in a strange apartment.
Lied and stole and cheated, blamed everyone else
        for the rot inside –

O litany of terrible deeds I don't
remember, which work still like a small machine
underneath memory. O litany
        of terrible deeds

I hope to see forgiven. O litany
of terrible deeds done against me I hope
to forgive. My mother helped me stand the bird bath
        back on its stone feet.

Fisting Sappho

Circa 630 BCE, in the city of Mytilene, on the island of Lesbos, a woman was born. Her parents, members of the city's nobility, were likely named Cleis and Scamandronymus, and she had three brothers: Eurygios, Larichos, and Charaxos. This woman was named Sappho.

She was a high priestess of the cult of Aphrodite and an educator of girls and women. She was "slanderously accused" of "shameful intimacy with certain of her female pupils."[1] This was, of course, false. She married and had a daughter, named after her mother Cleis, with Kerkylas of Andros.

Around 570 BCE, Sappho fell in love with a ferryman named Phaon, but her affections were unrequited. As Aphrodite was cured of her grief for Adonis by leaping from the Leucadian cliffs, Sappho followed in her footsteps. She did not survive the attempt. Renowned as a lyric poet in her own time, she remains in the canon of Greek poets to this day, though most of her work was lost to history.

Sappho is fucking me on a mattress on the floor of their parents' attic. They are home on a college break, and we're only in the same room once a month or so these days. When we do see each other, we make up for lost time, spend hours under each other's hands. I am begging into their mouth – *more more more* – when they say, "There isn't any more."

Years later, I will remember this. We will sit in a coffee shop in a new city. I will look down at the table at their pale, fine hands and be reminded of a winter night when I was still in high school. I'll be reminded how we tried so desperately to fit into one another.

In the attic, we both look down to see their fist disappear inside me, gloved in my body to the wrist. We laugh, a little incredulous. It will not last, but tonight we are hungry in love. One long kiss and we fall back into rhythm.

---

[1] This according to the Suda, or Souda, an encyclopedia of the ancient world dating back to the 10th Century.

Circa 630 BCE, in the city of Mytilene, on the island of Lesbos, a woman was born. Her parents, members of the city's nobility, were likely named Cleis and Scamandronymus, and she had three brothers: Eurygios, Larichos, and Charaxos. This woman was named Sappho.

She married and had a daughter, named after her mother Cleis, with Kerkylas of Andros. She was active as a poet until about 570 BCE. Renowned as a lyric poet in her own time, she remains in the canon of Greek poets to this day, though most of her work was lost to history.

At the same time, in the same city, there was a courtesan. This woman was also named Sappho. She wrote no poetry, but seduced a series of young men and women to their downfall. This Sappho fell in love with a ferryman named Phaon, but her affections were unrequited. Spurned by her love, she took her own life by leaping from the Leucadian cliffs.

The reputation of the courtesan Sappho has, throughout history, been a stain upon the name of the beloved lyric poet.

I don't think Charaxos is his real name, and I don't think his wife knows I'm here, but that is what he tells me. From his job as a construction foreman, he has sent messages all day. I am finally in his kitchen, kicking off my shoes, asking the cat's name.

There are toys and lube and poppers on the bed, a duvet he certainly didn't choose, that faux-Tuscan style all my friends' parents loved in 2007. I imagine the mirror affixed to the ceiling was his idea. I'm surprised when he starts slow, works his way up from one finger to two, two fingers to three, three fingers to a toy, a toy to four fingers.

By the time his hand slips into me completely, we are lost in it. For some reason I'm still surprised, how he and I become we, despite our necessary distances. After I finish, he doesn't ask me to reciprocate. He just wanders off to wash his hands, tells me I better head out soon. We will message a few more times (he'll even offer to take me skeet shooting), but this is our only meeting face to face.

Circa 630 BCE, in the city of Mytilene, on the island of Lesbos, a woman was born. Her parents, members of the city's nobility, were likely named Cleis and Scamandronymus, and she had three brothers: Eurygios, Larichos, and Charaxos. This woman was named Sappho.

She was a high priestess of the cult of Aphrodite and had a number of woman lovers. These lovers were named in many of her surviving poems. Legend claims she married a man named Kerkylas of Andros and that she took her own life for unrequited love of Phaon, a ferryman. These claims are unsupported in the historical record. [2]

In 600 BCE, she was exiled to Sicily, where she was active as a poet until about 570 BCE. Renowned as a lyric poet in her own time, she remains in the canon of Greek poets to this day, though most of her work was lost to history.

When I wake up the morning after, Cleis has disappeared from the hotel bed and there is a faint pink stain on the sheets. I believe the blood is mine − Cleis wears her acrylics just a little too long. I piece it together: there was a blunt in the parking lot, Hennessy and Mario Kart, Arbor Mist bottles, Eurygios taking a bong hit without so much as cracking a window. Cleis and I wound up alone, somehow, in the shower, then in the bed.

A distinct memory, framed in drunken tunnel vision: my fist closed inside Cleis' body, my name on her lips, her nails digging into my shoulders. She will get tired of me first and disappear back into the life she surfaced from, but even now: her red hair on the white sheets, the pink crescent moons on my shoulders, my hand still smelling of her. The little things she left behind with me, that I left behind with her. A trace of blood.

---

[2] Considering the name "Kerkylas of Andros" roughly translates to "Prick from the Isle of Man," these are likely fabrications designed to convince us of her heterosexuality.

Circa 630 BCE, in the city of Mytilene, on the island of Lesbos, a woman was born. Her parents, members of the city's nobility, were likely named Cleis and Scamandronymus, and she had three brothers: Eurygios, Larichos, and Charaxos. This woman was named Sappho.

She was a high priestess of the cult of Aphrodite and an educator of girls and women. She was "slanderously accused" of "shameful intimacy with certain of her female pupils." This was, of course, true. These lovers were named in many of her surviving poems.

Around 570 BCE, Sappho fell in love with a ferryman named Phaon, but her affections were unrequited. As Aphrodite was cured of her grief for Adonis by leaping from the Leucadian cliffs, Sappho followed in her footsteps. She did not survive the attempt. Renowned as a lyric poet in her own time, she remains in the canon of Greek poets to this day, though most of her work was lost to history.

"There's absolutely no way I could fist you," Kerkylas says, holding up a hand, broad and rough, chipped red nail polish and callouses. I keep forgetting if they're a plumber or an electrician, despite the fact that they never stop talking about themself. "Way too big to fit in anybody."

We are in their bedroom, in what they keep calling their "uncle's" apartment. We both know the man who lives here isn't their uncle, just like we know the sobriety coin that fell out of their bag isn't a friend's. Still, they tell half-truths, carefully angle each story.

They won't ever fist me, just like I won't ever fuck them, just like we won't ever really meet each other's friends. To this day, in my dreams, their face changes each time I see it.

Sappho's nine books of poetry, only written down after her death, are gone. Prior to 1895, the only fragments of Sappho remaining were quotes of her work recovered from other writers. Regardless of the scarcity of her work, women writers from the sixteenth century onward adopted her as their symbol, and men used her sordid reputation to disparage them.

After the discovery of the Oxyrhynchus papyri in Al-Bahnasa, Egypt, many more fragments of her work were uncovered. Over the course of the early twentieth century, her status as an icon for lesbians and women who love women solidified.

Sappho's reality is veiled from us by illiteracy, time, culture, interpretation. "Sappho's poems, composed 2,600 years ago, are with us still. Sappho's name is with us still. From the past she glimmers, and we remember. In the future she beckons, and we respond[3]."

On a twin bed in his mother's basement, Phaon puts the bottle of poppers to my nose and tells me to breathe deep. He doesn't know yet that I've been drunk for months, that I can feel it turning ugly inside me. I know we don't have much time left. He slides another finger in – *you can take it, baby, you can take it.*

But I can't. We flip positions, something changes – on top, I feel like I'm the one fucking him, that his body is full of me. I tell him so and we share this, feel together the way our bodies mingle somewhere beyond the physical.

We both come; the moment passes. I can still see myself on him, inside him, filled by him – connected by cords of pleasure, obscurity, care, pain. The only word that comes to mind is *glukupikron* – "sweet-bitter," as Sappho writes it.

---

[3] This from Margaret Reynolds' book, *The Sappho Companion.*

Sappho is a Lesbian. Sappho is a lesbian. Sappho is a doppelganger. Sappho is a palimpsest. Sappho is a right on woman. Sappho is a wife. Sappho is myth. Sappho is a tribade. Sappho is a courtesan. Sappho is a poet.

Sappho is a figure blurred in the distance, standing on the edge of the Leucadian cliffs. Sappho is a lover's fist opening inside your body, blooming invisible pleasure.

PIKRON

Leda / Swan

It's not rape when gods do it —
gods ravage, take, deflower,
seduce even — but not rape.

It feels like that when it happens,
like weather, like tides, awful
and ordinary. What counts

toward your pain? Who's allowed
to claim survival? I was drunk —
I only remember

after, the empty guilt
making a home below my ribs.
I laid in bed, counted

spokes on the ceiling fan
as they passed. The days went
and I forgot his face.

I wonder if Leda smiled
when she first opened her eyes
to feathers. I'm sure she knew

what could be borne, or stopped.
Even her terror passes through
rage, into something like grace.

Odysseus Leaving Aeaea

Before gin and tonics,
before dab hits and whippets,
before disappointing bareback

and fruit snack packets
with the sun coming up
and his migraine coming on,

I know this is the last time
I will see him. Never mind
whatever it is we thought

we had in common.
I'm the shame he tasted
a few sleepless hours,

he is the thing I have tried
to use as glue. He sleeps.
I read the texts from the breakup.

The drugs are free when you give
a lonely body what it asks.
I'll drive the hours home

windows open, radio loud –
I may as well deserve
whatever it is that's coming.

The Oracle at Bellevue

The devil made me shoot me in the mouth / and doctors
made a new jaw out of iron, / broke my mother's china and
filed shards / into gleaming teeth, razor wires, put them / in
my pink face like diamonds, rhinestones. / They stole a dead
man's lips and shut me up / in his red smile. I owe the GDP
/ of a medium-sized country settled / somewhere in the back
alleys of other / hemispheres, that "developing world," / that
black and white photograph we are not / supposed
to recognize the faces in. / Maybe I'll live long enough
to accumulate / cents and dollars to erase my name / from
their long memory – but no. I was dead / before bullet
left chamber, dead before gun / touched hand, dead before
the devil grinned / back at me from bumpers of expensive
cars. / Dead so long I couldn't tell you when or how / or who
– I am ash the color sand shines / over my stripped skull as
light sings through, / clay and carbon turning church window.
/ I am the sweet / decay, the lovely rot. / I am the sex
of eternal sleep / as it breathes through me. One day that wind
will rest, and I with it.

Unnamed Nymph #16 / Zeus

A man with a gun in his lap
sits beside what was once
a woman. It buckles

a belt, adjusts a collar.
On the dashboard between them
sits a scrap of metal, mirror.

This could belong to either (we know
it belongs to the man). The man
wants back what he has paid.

The not-woman is a snared fox.
Perhaps it can't speak (we know
it can). The man with a gun

in his lap takes a stack
of damp bills from it's
open hand, counts them.

The man drives toward his wife.
The not-woman disappears,
street-lamp blinks out overhead.

The man's wife waits, patient
as a heron. The not-woman
does not speak for a long time.

Athenian Ritual

I have been losing weight.
Once, he gripped skeins of fat
bound in skin, left trails

of purpled fingerprints –
wine dark, saccharine – up
the thighs. Now his hips

bruise against bone.
The body is a simple weapon
if you learn how to use it.

It is easy to disappear.
Stand in front of the mirror,
no guard on the trimmer, let

hair gather at my ankles.
I will drink until sleep
and it will not hurt to smile.

I will feel the night cold
on my new clean scalp, against
the bruises under my cheek.

I will leave the loose hair
on the cold tile. I will burn
this house down, both of us in it.

Medusa / Athena

His wife calls to say
people like me
could put the devil

out of work. *Better*
him than me, I think,
bet he's got a pension.

Her husband smells of salt,
stale office heat,
whatever he ate last,

and I want to tell her this,
open him up to her,
a surgical diagram.

I want to tell
the truth: I'm the snake
eating its own tail.

I want her to know she
cast a shadow in their bed,
homely perfume sick on skin –

I just thank her. Step out, light
a cigarette, wait
while nicotine stills the hands.

Crossing Lethe

It's just past sunrise when
I park in the driveway,
vomit in a snowbank.

Mom is asleep when
my untied hands find
themselves in her kitchen,

setting the kettle to boil,
testing first sober hours.
I can't brush my teeth,

can't eat a slice of toast,
can't hold my phone, can't sleep
or apologize. I wait

a while, stand at the kitchen
window, watch cardinals
fight over remnants

in ice. My hands – old hands,
dry-mud cracked and pale – reflect
early light, vibrate. Slow

to work the peel off clementines,
section after section to my mouth
until nothing's left but skin.

Clytemnestra / Agamemnon

Watch him count the cash between
us. I can smell it. Thick
smoke between blue eyes

and bifocals, Cuban clutched
in chiclet teeth. He folds
the stack of clean bills

between my lips. *Good boy.*
Snubs stuttering ember out
against the shoulder.

His eyes, wet coins; my own still
face doubled, quadrupled
in glass, gloss, glaviaux.

He sinks to his knees,
buries his face in my empty
lap, slick spit and tears.

Watch: I brush salt and coal
hair from shining temples,
imagine I could sink

fingers into the neck,
soft as a thigh. Listen
to the gasp, gag – then quiet.

Actaeon / Hounds

He died on a Thursday night,
strung by a belt from the bar
in the closet-turned-goon-cave.

The closet was contested
territory – his wife
insisted he keep it locked,

even while inside, in case
their son dropped in (he never did).
He did all his hangings here

perched on the edge of a stool,
assumed the bar would not hold
his weight, but when the stool slipped,

it did. His wife missed him
the next morning, called the fire
department to remove him

with axes like a girl inside
a fairy tale wolf, but he
was long dead by then.

The last thing he saw were empty
eyes of pup masks lined like soldiers
along the opposite shelf.

grindr chat

NARCISSUS

i am: bi dl not gen. u should be: clean smooth obedient. do u bb?
pnp? can't host my son lives – no not in public not with the cops
around here. i am so lonely i could – hotel? 17 south
ramsey there's a spot. i want to make – want to own that – pics?
whatever u have. does it ever make u gag? no i mean just all
of it. here's what i'm going to do to – what too much?
u mad at me honey? what did i say that hasn't been said? what did i
say that u haven't thought? we all just want someone to swallow
us. now don't be like that. all the same. we r only animals
and anyway i've got favors. there that's my boy – daddy's little – good
– but – no? maybe another time.

AMEINIAS

will u fuck me if i beg? what if i ask real nice? what if u don't
have to wear a condom? what if u don't have to look
me in the eye? host or travel? i live with family sorry – car stuff?
i get off at six. no just my mom. what if i ask u to ruin me?
make me nothing? what a relief to be what i'm told. is it hard
to believe u aren't the first to suffer? some days i think it impossible.
if i let u come inside will u give me a line, a hit
of something? will u fill me with whatever u can find? what will we
have that we didn't start with? will u pull the hurt out of me when u
go? tie it to ur bumper, hit the gas, i will wait here for this bleeding
to stop. looking? what for?

Eurydice / Orpheus

Route 80 again, as far
as I can drive, coffee, back
the way I came. Nights full

of an itch I thought I outgrew.
Between us a tenderness
torn along its edges.

We sound for the catch,
what each can't love of the other
(the truth: I can't stand to be

loved). I say half honest
things in bed, hope you'll hear
through me. You split me open

(you are beautiful). Outside
roadkill, sumac, mile markers,
an empty I'd slip into

like silk (you'd never find me).
I love you (this will hurt
us). A whip of hair

and cigarette ash, I pass
like neon highway signs.
Look again (I'm gone).

CRETAN
INTERLUDE

after sculpture by H. Highwater

Part I: Asterion

Like all monsters, born and built
to teach some man some lesson
without worry for who lives

in the new body. No
script written for you so
no one taught you to speak,

but you grew up in dark,
sturdy and white as ghost pipe,
spindly limbs turned to muscle.

You were still calf-awkward
when they set you running into
that great cage. The wet-black eyes

set apart by your wide
wooly forehead blinked the dark
away. You found yourself

bleating alone between marble
walls painted with scenes
of some other prince's life.

One day an Athenian
your age will drop a piece of chalk.
You don't know how to write so

you will draw stars
between blood stains on the floor,
remember songs and hours

from your first night here –
how you wondered what the feast
was for, how you tapped the bell

around your neck in time.
It takes some years
to learn you are a monster.

In the meantime, press
your warm body into cold
corners, gasp a calf's milk breath

into your human palms,
imagine a green place to sleep
quiet, save for soft talk elsewhere.

Pasiphae / White Bull

So easy to surrender
under you, easy to slip
beneath us into your want.

When I can't remember why
I spent that summer on a leash
of your attention, remember

your whimper in the dark,
your eyes wide and glossy
while you begged. Our bodies hot

from the sun, how could I
refuse you when I made
myself for you to want?

Somehow all along we knew
we were part of a process,
a putting ourselves back

together. Still, the night.
The lengths we went to please
each another. Still, the beach

where we stood knee deep and watched
the sun rise. We were not afraid,
knowing how soon it would end.

Part II: A Crack in the Labyrinth

The hole began as a crack,
became a divot, was made
a place to sharpen your horns

until – air – light – color.
At first you avoid it, then
won't leave its side, face pressed

to stone trying to look
further even though you know
you can't. This is how you learn –

bird – blue – cypress – cloud – sun –
breeze. You shun it for weeks
when children from town throw stones,

sing songs, taunt the opening,
but children get bored and years
go by. No one notices

you blinking in the shadows.
For weeks, a girl stands just
below your line of vision

and sings lullabies at dusk.
She's always alone, she always
comes when the sky is touched pink,

she's always quiet so you
must swivel your ears to catch
the familiar words – someone

faceless and warm sang these songs
in the place you were before,
the place the girl must come from.

When she calls you brother you try
to answer but your lowing
only frightens her away.

She doesn't return the next night
and you abandon the crack
until you think you can forget

the girl's voice – but it is still there
caught in the top of the cypress
a little taller each night.

Knossos, New Jersey

Follow concentric circles,
cul-de-sacs, side streets lined
with identical low roofs,

no power lines or tall trees,
just hydrangea and bay laurel
closing off cracked sidewalks.

My family loves me, sure,
but it's hard to know
a beast who can't tell you

what it needs. My sister's friend
tells us *you just have to find
a man who wants you a little*

more than you want him. Her eyes
are dark enough we don't
contradict her. Somewhere off

this street there are swans – they hiss
if you come too near their clutch
of eggs. One cygnet might survive,

only to vanish into
the wide winter, abandon
its parents to what they chose.

Part III: The Stars, At Last

When the hero comes you laugh,
a sound you haven't heard
yourself make before. He follows

his thread between rooms, seeks
you where you rest at the heart.
Maybe tomorrow you

will be dead – you hear him come
and you are tired of this
story, tired of being

the necessary villain.
Your sister has given you
this (love, after a fashion)

and your mother feels fooled
by your father and you were
born into what they are – you,

proxy sacrifice, you,
body left to bleed, you,
dragged into moonlight

by your mantle of white horns.
It's your first time seeing
the whole night sky. You

turn your head toward a salt breeze,
turn your back on the hero
to savor this first free breath

of bloodless air. In the morning
maybe it will be over.
Maybe you'll leave two footprints

behind you on the path north.
Maybe the city will glimpse
your broad furred shoulders

one last time, your bell cut loose
from its frayed cord. Feel the sun
on your bare chest, it too a star

making a piece of someone
else's constellation, somewhere
you are finally headed.

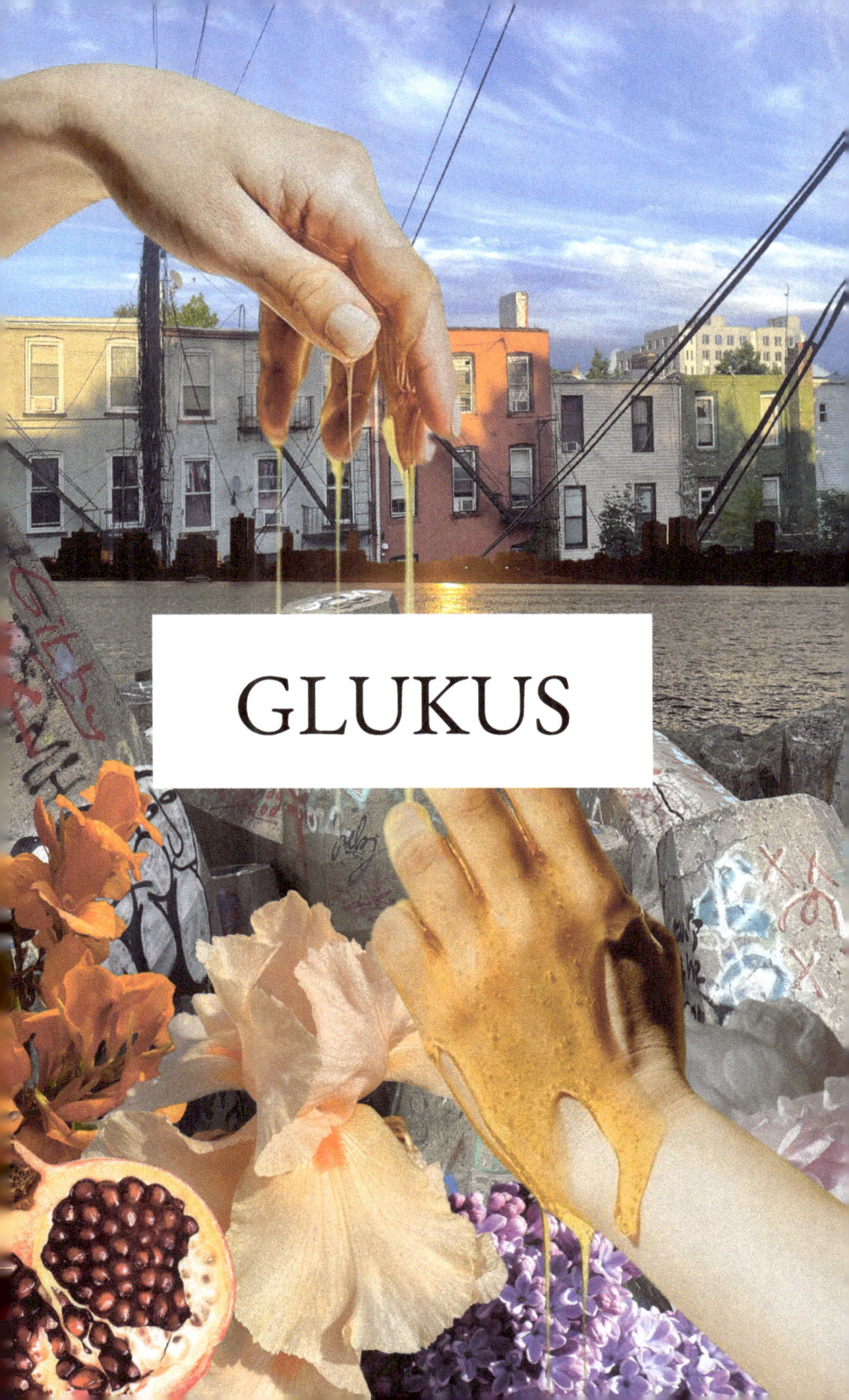

GLUKUS

Echo After Zeus

Wanted to say no – instead
said yes, said please, said of course,
said don't listen when I say

stop – wanted to safeword but
said nothing. Prided myself
on how well I took what I

would not let myself refuse
you (everything, anything).
You were good to me after,

made sure I wasn't hurt, held
me close. You asked if I was
pleased comfortable tired

and I was pleased comfortable
tired, asked if what we had done
was good for me and what we

had done was good for me.
You only ever hurt me
when I asked you to, but I

learn now how to ask without
my parrot voice – all sound
without sense – all yes – no – yes –

Helen of Boonville

for Helen Manzer

Before the handsome air force
husband who drank and hit;
before the two children who

stopped speaking to each other
when she died; before the white
wrought iron furniture and

the white Pontiac and
the white stones in the yard
she painted herself; before

even the apartment
in Manhattan, painting
her nails, a scarf over the lamp

during air raid drills; before
there was a woman there was
a girl. Her teeth a little

crooked, her nose a little
hooked. Her mother warned her
against the boys' automobiles.

She looked for a long time
past the dairy farm's borders
out past sight to where the world was.

Persephone / Hades

I knew men a moment
I may have loved, if
we weren't both brief creatures.

I'll never see the earring
I lost in his sheets again, but
I have some hours to hold

when we touched. My laugh open-
mouthed, him undressed of his black.
We ate slow summer things

in bed, bare skinned, shared
fruit from sticky hands
and begged seeds to root

bitter-dark inside us.
Heat held between open
palms. No lover, just

a long night we forgot
anything but pleasure
in borrowed hours after

one shift, before the next.
I carry his voice, sleep thick
in my ear, bodies left behind.

Achilles and Patroclus After the Riot Police

Beloved cleans beloved's
blood and grease paint from eyes,
corners of chapped lips.

White cloth, warm water,
a little soap. The boy king
of Newark sits on the edge

of the bathtub, his lover
on his knees before him,
supplicant, acolyte.

Each cleans and bandages
the other's wounds, careful
to be gentle when they can,

and our hero follows
his lionheart to bed
still unmade from morning.

Each falls asleep, listens
to the quiet voice inside
this other man, the rumble.

Intimate machinery
of bodies trying
to keep themselves alive.

Hermes / Peitho

The woman whose bones
became part of someone else
and, when he opened her black

vinyl bag, she was crumpled,
a discarded garment
pooled at her own feet.

Often their blank eyes
wouldn't close, so he sealed them
with glue or fine white thread.

Little punctures dotted
his fingertips where needles
full of formaldehyde slipped

and caught his living skin.
My body warmed his bed.
I drew out his rougher

touch, helped him discard respect
he took such pride in. After,
he skimmed rough palms over

my flesh as it cooled, and I
imagined myself trusted
to him, like the precious dead.

Cassandra at the Library

She walks in all faggot
swagger, glittering rags,
finest the NYU

dorm dumpsters
have to offer after
encampments and final

exams – denim skirt,
some metallic fabric
wrapped intricately around

her tanned torso. She smiles,
asks my name, if we have
anything by the Delphic

Oracle or Nora Roberts.
Not soft but wiry, taught-muscled,
keen-eyed and sure as anyone

who must be to survive.
On the way out she offers
a wink of recognition.

She knows a simple thing –
I'm close to her. We both
live in the mouths of lions.

Anacreon of Hackensack

One shot for Matthew Shepard,
one for me, customary
for the weekend crowd of younger,
more beautiful men. I wear
a ring with a pink triangle,
a wedding band to my left.
One shot for Leelah Alcorn,
one for me, and we step onto
the sidewalk. A driver slows
to shout from his window what
I am – I can't help but smile,
wish I could whisper in his ear,
this man who named me on sight,
old friend. I want to tell him
exactly the flame this kindling
body could light. I want
to tell him I could burn
the empty from his stomach
if only he'd let me try.

Penelope / Odysseus

You went to the orgy alone
but I still caught your cold.
Well, one must imagine

Penelope happy.
For a week you, me, and all
the hottest transsexuals

in Brooklyn sneeze into elbows,
eat acetaminophen
like candy, sleep until two.

You show me pictures of dark
rooms, bodies transfigured
into unlikely shapes,

and I understand that this
is part of the pleasure –
come home and I am still

here. Watch me watch you bent
beneath some stranger, not
broken, not lost – wandering.

Lover, I don't mind
how long that train home takes
so long as you are on it.

Bacchus, Bronx

Stoned, they take their time, open
my body, rough tender,
intent on want. We sprawl

on the unmade bed, clothes
scattered. It takes some time
for me to lean into our

bodies, their touch, animal
fear rising out of habit.
Full of their hands, I beg –

please – please – please – pant desire.
Our bodies move together
through my fear into frenzy –

I bite into the fresh meat
of sturdy shoulders, cling
to their bulk, lose my mind

a little. What's that line?
I feel guilty about all
my pleasures – but looking down

the long gray cylinder
of fate, I won't regret
saying their name again – again.

Hyacinthus / Apollo

I spent that summer in bed
with a ghost – early sober,
no ID, no bank account,

no condoms, two ex-wives.
He fucked like an animal
and cried. We cruised Palisades

Parkway to the overlook,
parked among fogged windows
and walked to the edge to see

the city – like television
for dogs – big fields and rabbits.
We drove down route 46,

flooded between barricades,
since he had to shoot pool
in a hurricane and I

couldn't keep my mouth off him
in the dark lot. We drove
to Lodi, Englewood, Garfield,

down the shore. We drove windows
open, hands all over, lit
each cigarette off the end

of the last. We kissed hard
over the parking brake. He tied
me to his bed and I pulled

so hard I broke the chain.
I spent that summer eating
in bad restaurants, sent videos

from strangers' rooms, listened
to 90s club stories, mistook
pleasure for happiness.

We drove once to the reservoir.
I watched water darken
as he whispered into my neck –

come on, baby – don't you want
the story of the summer
you spent with me in Jersey?

Astraeus / Eos

The projector sprays blue stars
against the door, bookshelves, pictures.
Window open, neighborhood

sounds low and steady. I play
with your fingers, we take turns
with my pipe, breathe in, out, watch –

smoke moves through light, becomes air.
By the time you fall asleep,
your face against my shoulder,

light, smoke, open window
make one breath – the night.
Your temples collect pools

of sweat in their small bowls,
your brow furrows some dreamed need
or worry you won't remember

when I ask over eggs,
potatoes, spam, coffee.
Tonight, the breeze moves smoke

over your face, closed in sleep.
I'll spend a few more hours here
with our bodies, this mystery.

Muse Prayer

"I started with people much more talented than me…and they're dead or in jail or not writing. The difference between me and them is that I'm writing."
- Alexander Chee, paraphrasing Annie Dillard

Four years after I thought
I'd written my way out
of my own myth – a year

without a single poem –
and three years drafting my way
back to the page – I return

to the altar every night
for weeks. I light incense
and try again to ask

for a new way to speak.
For years I thought you would never
reach out for me again.

A new friend asks *didn't you*
used to write poems? The shame
comes, though I can't tell if

I'm embarrassed to be
a failed poet or to have tried
to write poems at all.

Then you come down out of light
and history to remind me
what it is I have to lose.

THE
CAE
NEID

Caeneus Redux

Sure, it's an ugly story,
no uglier than any
story told as if true

about last days
in fated bodies. Sure,
it's an everyday terror,

like an interstate pile up,
a field of twisted metal,
but I am tired

of tearing at my own seams,
trying to pull out what was done
with my body while I looked

elsewhere. I can't change it,
just the way it's carried.
I stood for a long while

at the edge of the water.
I didn't step away when
waves fell over my feet.

I let the tide come in
up to my knees, certain
it would not move me.

Caenis in Thessaly

Nothing left here, but how
to leave? I know nothing
of the world, myself, this body,

how it becomes unwatched.
As a child I climbed trees.
I stole bags of cherries

into dogwood's top branches,
spit jewel pits onto the street,
smeared stained fingers on jeans.

It was the summer before
my body turned sour,
began to take, not give,

bleed, warp, call out
wants I couldn't answer
or name. I wasn't afraid

then. That's all I ask for:
piss scent of dogwood blossoms,
leathered supermarket

cherries kept too long on ice.
A child's mindless calm, no fear
of the threat inherent to height.

Caenis / Elatus

My father taught me never
turn your back on water.
He took me fishing –

only caught and kept once,
a rainbow trout someplace
in Connecticut. Scales

stuck iridescent
to our hands, long thin blade
of a knife used for nothing

else. The fish in its shroud
of foil, thin bones pulled
translucent from white flesh.

To kill it, he beat the trout's
head against a flat, hot rock.
He had me close my eyes.

The sound of the body
on stone. One eye opening
despite his warning –

too bright to see anything
in light reflected off
wide white water.

Caenis / Poseidon

Before I knew the ocean
could hurt me, I threw myself
full-bodied into it

every chance I got. It took
a long time to go wrong,
but it's never clever

to put yourself in hands
that could unmake you. I think
it was off Cape Cod – turned

away from the water,
maybe to watch a kite ride
wind up the sky, maybe

to answer someone's calling.
A wave hit the back of my knees,
another took me under,

and I turned over in that green –
blue – white – until human hands
pulled me onto sand. I'm still

under all that water. I
am sand – not made what I am
by tides, but molded.

Caenis / Caeneus

It's been a long season since
a dead, wet room opened in me.
Too hot showers, stubble,

a stranger's teeth, tongue, rough palms,
damp hair, dirty fingernails.
Spit in the sink, tie back your hair,

wash your hands – this the frenzy
of getting by, life as we
know it. I let a doctor

open my body, take out
something young, soft, defenseless.
My mother always called it

developing, like a photo
in a chemical bath –
all it needed was some light.

That was another growth though,
under a different sun.
It's been a long season since

prayers against shower tiles,
grinding teeth in the night,
sweat-soaked sheets on the floor.

Caenis' Metamorphosis

Magic thing – a surgeon's knife.
I went to sleep burdened with
his son and woke incapable

of motherhood. A kingly
gift – godly – to sleep like death
and come to bleeding, sure

you've removed the part of you
most easily snared. The first
time I lost a woman's shape,

gained a few scars, nothing
which couldn't be borne by this
new sturdy body. I burst

seams, popped buttons with the great
cask of my chest. The second time
I bled and bled for weeks, fell

under the knife again, swore
it was some trick you'd played – then
it passed like a storm on open

water. Still there was his son,
the size of a penny, heart
drumming with mine, until –

Caeneus / Elatus

After chemotherapy
my father and I watch
Antiques Roadshow, try to guess

the estimates: Civil War
era Union flag, doll
made by Wisconsin pioneers,

a little Greek sculpture brought
back by some grandfather
from some war. We're not good

at guessing, but games pass time
and take his mind off pain
that overflows the hours.

Today he is curious –
do testosterone injections
hurt? Do people treat me well

at work? Are the men I see
gay or straight? Don't they mind my –
well, he means well. Some things, though,

he thinks he wants to know
are best left unsaid. He will
forget, by morning, he asked.

Caeneus, King of the Lapiths

Everybody laughs at my jokes
and everybody stares at my ass
and everybody loves when I

tell stories about my days
chasing centaurs off cliffs,
landing on both feet.

I look sexy when I yawn
and I am good at everything
and no one tells me otherwise –

no one dares tell me a thing –
at least not to my face. I leave
rooms with all the air. No one

would guess how deep it goes,
this layer of bitter shine –
that's why they eat their meals

right from my hands, warm teeth
chip against my fingers.
Everybody loves me when

my mouth and my legs are open,
and everybody laughs and
laughs and laughs and laughs –

Caeneus / Latreus

Before desire turned on me,
I was held loose in a lover's
fist. There was a time I might

have refused what my body
asked of me. The phone rings
from another room, asks me

to abandon the body.
Come live a moment
in this choice I made – don't

let me forget I made it.
The man in my phone
(it is always almost

the same man) wants me
restrained, unspeaking, trussed
for slaughter. I am not

a needful thing. Once I may
have thought twice, but I don't have
to think much these days.

Like all good soldiers, I know
I have a simple task: if
I go down, bring him with me.

Centauromachy

It's easy to be free
when you can't be touched, easy
to be loved and risk nothing,

but he asked me to open
myself, to lower a mask
I'd forgotten I wore.

I found I could not bear it.
After all, you can't give
back divine gifts, even when

they sour, so many old grapes.
I'll miss my body clothed
in his tenderness, nights we

held like water in our bowl
of hands, but I am not
a man who knows how to slip

the leash he's caught himself in.
I bought safety at the cost
of joy, and there's only so

much pressure a body can take.
What refuses to bend always
breaks beneath its own weight.

Caeneus / Poseidon

Heat drives us into water
in herds – sun beats sand,
reflects off waves, presses our skin

against us until we reach
out for the sea's cold hand.
It's not so hot on Labor Day,

our last Riis trip this season,
and I wander off to
walk into the waves alone,

slip between the bodies lined
just past the place waves break.
As the water crests, I close

my eyes, slip beneath salt,
each time surfacing to breath,
sun, voices, water

blinking out along
the horizon. I go under,
stay a long time, eyes open

to a green that doesn't end.
A good day, gentle surf.
I let it carry me awhile.

Caeneus' Metamorphosis

Retired from slut – new career
in sad. You wouldn't dare
say hello on the street,

I am so some other beast
than the one you knew. I shed
you like a skin, sweetheart.

I wear my new face in daylight,
I eat fruit in single bites,
I am learning flight again.

When I was a girl,
I was afraid. When I was
a man, I was numb. When I

come back from the dead, I will
be something different. It may
be worse, it may be better,

but it will – it will – be new.
If you're looking for me look
out of the corner of your eye.

If you're looking for me look
for the warbler rising out
of smoke on the horizon.

NOTES

p. 7 | Mythweaver

Anne Carson translates the word "μυθοπλόκος" as "mythweaver," stating it as a name the Greek lyric poet Sappho used for Eros, in her translation, *If Not, Winter*.

The fall of Icarus is a story you've likely heard some version of if you've heard any Greek myths. Daedalus is imprisoned by King Minos after the events of the Minotaur story (which you can read more about under "Cretan Interlude") with his son, Icarus. Daedalus, an inventor and craftsman, builds wings for him and his son to escape with. Icarus, however, doesn't listen to his father's advice not to fly too close to the sun. The sun melts the beeswax holding the feathers onto Icarus' wings, and he falls to his death in the sea.

As mentioned in the epigraph, Pieter Bruegel the Elder's painting "Landscape with the Fall of Icarus" inspired this poem.

pp. 10-17 | The Erotes

Aphrodite, infamous goddess of love, has an entourage of minor deities, the Erotes, each associated with a different kind of love:

- Eros: general god of love, including sex and fertility
- Anteros: god of requited love, avenger of unrequited love
- Phthonus: god of jealousy and envy
- Hymen: god of marriage and weddings
- Himeros: god of desire and unrequited love
- Hermaphroditus: where we get the word hermaphrodite, god/ess of gender fuckery (and child of Hermes and Aphrodite)
- Pothos: god of longing and yearning
- Hedylogos: god of sweet talk and flattery

p. 20 | The Other Sappho

Most of what you need to know about Sappho is in the essay "Fisting Sappho" – including the fact that, throughout history, people have theorized that there were "two Sapphos" on the island of Lesbos. One was a respectable educator and poet, and the other was somehow both a lesbian and a courtesan who killed herself over a man. The theory of the two Sapphos has, thankfully, been discarded over the years.

p. 21 | Ganymede / Zeus

Ganymede, a Trojan youth, is taking care of his sheep when he is abducted by a giant eagle. The eagle is either under the direction of, or just is, Zeus. Zeus grants Ganymede eternal youth and immortality, and brings him to live on Mount Olympus as the cup-bearer of the gods. This is not the sort of job offer one has the capacity to decline.

pp. 22-23 | Labors of Heracles

Heracles got an extensive rebranding by the Romans as Hercules, and you can probably fill in a few details about his infant career in snake-strangling, his eventual divine ascension, and his beautiful wife, Megara. Sadly, Megara and Heracles don't have so happy an ending in the myth as they do in the Disney film.

Hera, Zeus' wife, hates Heracles because he is Zeus' son by a mortal woman, Alcmene. Hera drives Heracles to madness, and he kills Megara and their children. When he recovers from his madness and sees what he's done, he asks the Oracle at Delphi (who you can learn more about in the entry for "The Oracle at Bellevue") how to repent. She tells him to serve King Eurystheus, who sets twelve labors for him to complete. When he completes the labors despite all odds, he is forgiven and made immortal.

The Sappho quote is from Anne Carson's translation of fragment 5 from her complete translation of Sappho's work, *If Not, Winter*.

pp. 24-29 | Fisting Sappho

All of the stories told about Sappho in this essay are stories told about her throughout history. We have absolutely no way of knowing what is true. She remains a significant figure for queer women, and a giant of poetry in general. The Margaret Reynolds book referenced, *The Sappho Companion*, is a great source of knowledge about her if your curiosity is piqued.

p. 32 | Leda / Swan

Leda is a Spartan queen, wife of Tyndareus, and she is either seduced or raped (depending on who you ask) by Zeus in the form of a swan. She lays two eggs, one of which hatches her twin children by her husband, Clytemnestra and Castor, and one of which hatches her twin children by Zeus, Helen and Pollux.

p. 33 | Odysseus Leaving Aeaea

Odysseus is (shockingly) the central figure in Homer's Odyssey. After fighting for ten years in the Trojan War, it takes Odysseus ten more years to make his way home to Ithaca. Along the way, he spends a year on the island of Aeaea with the sorceress/goddess Circe.

p. 34 | The Oracle at Bellevue

The Oracle at Delphi, whose name this poem's title plays on, was the high priestess of the Temple of Apollo in Delphi. She oversaw the Temple, as well as acting as a source of prophecy, future telling, and general wise advice for people across ancient Greece. There were other oracles, but if someone in Greek myth is seeking one out, it's probably the Delphic Oracle.

Bellevue Hospital is now part of the NYC Health + Hospitals public health system in New York City, though it has been in operation since 1736. It is a comprehensive hospital, but its reputation for treating psychiatric patients has made its name into a pejorative shorthand for any psychiatric hospital.

p. 35 | Unnamed Nymph #16 / Zeus

Zeus has a habit of sexually assaulting pretty much any woman he happens to be attracted to, much to his wife Hera's ire (and, I'm sure, the other women's). There is not any particular story that inspired this piece, but there are many stories like it.

p. 36 | Athenian Ritual

Athenians wore their hair long in childhood, and cutting it short was a solemn ritual undertaken when boys came into young adulthood.

p. 37 | Medusa / Athena

The origins of the gorgons (the name given to the kind of creature Medusa is) vary from story to story, and gorgoneia (Gorgon heads painted or carved onto walls, shields, and other flat surfaces that may warrant protecting) predate the Medusa story. There are some versions of the story where Medusa and her two sisters, Stheno and Euryale, are monsters, but in earlier Greek depictions they're beautiful, if terrifying, women. The three sisters' power to turn men into stone with a single look is a common theme, though. In most versions, Medusa is the only sister who is mortal, and she is beheaded in her sleep by Perseus, who then uses her head's petrifying quality to kill many, many people.

It's not until the Roman poet Ovid that Medusa's story takes on the shape of so many stories in the Metamorphoses. Medusa is a beautiful young woman and, as so often happens in the Metamorphoses, she is raped by Poseidon (called Neptune by the Romans) in a temple to Athena (called Minerva by the Romans). Athena punishes Medusa for Poseidon's transgression, turning her beautiful hair to snakes and making her into a gorgon.

p. 38 | Crossing Lethe
The River Lethe is one of the rivers that runs through Hades, the Underworld. When the deceased drank the waters of the river, it erased the memories of their lives on earth.

p. 39 | Clytemnestra / Agamemnon
There are a few versions of the story about how Agamemnon dies at the hands of his wife, Clytemnestra. Here's one: Agamemnon returns from the sack of Troy with his war bride, Cassandra (see "Cassandra at the Library"), and it's been more than ten years since he left. This has given Clytemnestra a lot of time to think about their daughter, Iphigenia, who Agamemnon sacrificed to Artemis to ensure his and his men's safe passage to Troy. Clytemnestra has taken up with Agamemnon's cousin in the meantime, and they conspire to murder Agamemnon as vengeance for the death of her daughter. There are versions where Agamemnon comes off even worse, having killed Clytemnestra's first husband and son before forcing her to marry him.

p. 40 | Actaeon / Hounds
Actaeon was an accomplished hunter until he stumbled upon Artemis bathing. Artemis, famously-unwed dyke-goddess of hunting and the moon, turns him into a stag as revenge. In some versions of the story, the hounds that kill him and tear him apart are Artemis' – but I like Ovid's version, where Actaeon's own hounds destroy their master, then chase his scent through the woods, desperate to find him.

p. 41 | grindr chat
Grindr is a gay hook up app that shows users' profiles based on proximity (the distance given from the nearest profile is usually in feet). Narcissus was a hunter renowned for his beauty, but he rejected all suitors. Eventually, he caught sight of his own reflection in a stream and (being renowned for his

beauty and not his brains) fell in love with himself. He was so entranced that he withered away and died right there on the bank of the stream, and daffodils (also known as narcissus) sprouted up where his body lay. In some versions of this story, Narcissus is cursed to this fate, or more generally to never have his love returned. Nemesis, the goddess of revenge, puts this curse into motion at the behest of Ameneias, a young man infatuated with Narcissus but, like all his other suitors, rejected by him.

p. 42 | Eurydice / Orpheus

Eurydice dies by snake bite on her wedding day, and her husband, the poet Orpheus, travels to the Underworld to retrieve her. Once he gets to the Underworld, he plays and sings so beautifully that even the dead weep. Hades (in most versions at the behest of his wife, Persephone, see "Persephone / Hades") says that Orpheus may leave with his wife, but she must follow behind him and he must not turn to look at her. As they near the surface, Orpheus becomes convinced that he's been tricked, and turns just in time to see Eurydice disappear back into the Underworld. He tries to return to Hades to beg for another chance, but to no avail. How Eurydice feels about all this is less clear.

pp. 46-53 | Cretan Interlude

The story of Asterion, or the Minotaur, begins before the creature is born. King Minos receives a snow-white bull from Poseidon, but Minos fails to sacrifice the bull as directed. As punishment, Aphrodite bewitches Pasiphae, Minos' wife, into falling in love with the bull. Pasiphae asks Daedalus (of Daedalus and Icarus fame, see "Mythweaver") to build her a wooden cow suit that she can wear to mate with the white bull. She does, eagerly and successfully. She gives birth to Asterion, the Minotaur, who has a human body and a bull's head, and cares for him until he becomes too unruly to live in the palace in Knossos. Minos has Daedalus build a Labyrinth to contain Asterion nearby.

The Athenians are conscripted to provide seven young noble women and men every few years to be sacrificed to Asterion in the Labyrinth. This tribute is extracted from Athens as revenge for the death of Minos' (fully human) son.

When the third group of Athenians are called, Theseus, prince of Athens, is among them, with the promise to his father to kill the Minotaur. Ariadne, Pasiphae and Minos' daughter, falls in love with Theseus and gives him a thread to help him retrace his steps out of the Labyrinth. Theseus kills Asterion and sets off for his triumphant return to Athens, Ariadne in tow.

Hellen Highwater's "Old Stories" sculpture series was the 3D juried winner of the 2024 ArtPrize. "Part I: Asterion," "Part II: A Crack in the Labyrinth," and "Part III: The Stars, At Last" are titled after and inspired by Highwater's sculptures.

This poem is also indebted to Spencer Krug as Moonface's album, "This One's for the Dancer & This One's for the Dancer's Bouquet," which also retells Asterion's myth from his perspective.

p. 56 | Echo After Zeus

Zeus has a habit of chasing after nymphs, minor nature deities who seem to have spent most of their time trying to avoid being sexually assaulted by gods and satyrs. Hera, Zeus' wife, also has an unfortunate habit of blaming the women her husband assaults (or seduces, sometimes) for his actions. Echo is one such nymph who Hera takes revenge on – when Hera discovers her with Zeus, she curses her to be unable to say anything but the last words spoken to her. This becomes a particular issue when she falls in love with Narcissus and has to watch as he meets his fate (see "grindr chat" for more on him).

p. 57 | Helen of Boonville

Helen of Troy – the face that launched a thousand ships, as they say – is most famous for her role in the Trojan War, the subject matter of the Iliad and the Odyssey. Clytemnestra's (much more forgiving) sister, Helen is originally Helen of Sparta and wife of King Menelaus. However, she is either abducted by or runs away with Paris of Troy.

Helen Manzer, later Helen Dages, was my maternal grandmother. She was born on a dairy farm in Boonville, New York, in 1917 and died in a split-level ranch in New Jersey in 2003.

p. 58 | Persephone / Hades

Hades is the god of the dead and the king of the Underworld. Persephone is daughter of Demeter, goddess of the harvest, and one day she is abducted by Hades from a field where she's picking flowers with her friends. Hades forces her to stay with him in the Underworld as his wife, so her mother Demeter invents winter to punish the whole world (or at least Greece) for Hades' crime. Zeus eventually gives in and convinces Hades to return Persephone to earth so Demeter will allow the crops to grow. Hades either tricks Persephone into eating or forces her to eat six pomegranate seeds before she leaves. Based on the rules of the Underworld (which no one bothered to tell Persephone), this means she has to spend six months out of the year in Hades.

p. 59 | Achilles and Patroclus After the Riot Police

Achilles is the focal character of the Iliad and Greek hero of the Trojan War. He's hot, he's strong, and he'll tie your body to his chariot and ride in circles around your city walls if you kill his boyfriend. That boyfriend is Patroclus, and he is Achilles' companion throughout the Iliad before he is killed by the leader of the Trojans, Hector. Achilles takes his revenge, as I've mentioned, by tying Hector's corpse to his chariot and riding it around the walls of Troy for a few days. Theirs is a relationship often historically framed as a legendary friendship, but more recent interpretations tend towards romance.

p. 60 | Hermes / Peitho

Herald of the gods, Hermes is also the god of public speaking, thieves, merchants, and travelers. His job I'm concerned with here, though, is that of psychopomp, the guide that leads recently deceased souls from their bodies to the afterlife. While Hermes has lots of women, mortal and divine, he has children with, his wife is Peitho, goddess and personification of persuasion.

p. 61 | Cassandra at the Library

Cassandra is a Trojan princess, sister of Hector, and priestess of Apollo. Apollo offers Cassandra the power of prophecy if she'll go to bed with him. However, once the gift is bestowed, she backtracks and refuses his advances. There's no takesies-backsies on divine gifts, so, instead of removing her abilities, Apollo curses her to never be believed. There are some versions without Apollo's wrath – if not him, then snakes give her the double-edged gift.

You can find out more about the Delphic Oracle, referenced across stanzas four and five, in the entry for "The Oracle at Bellevue." Nora Roberts is a contemporary romance novelist.

p. 62 | Anacreon of Hackensack

Anacreon was an ancient Greek poet known best for drinking songs and erotic lyric poetry.

Matthew Shepard was a gay man brutalized and left to die tied to a fence in Laramie, Wyoming, in 1998. He was in a coma by the time he was discovered eighteen hours after the attack and he died on October 12, six days later, at 21 years old.

Leelah Alcorn was a transgender girl from Ohio. On December 28, 2014, citing her parents' rejection of her trans identity, she committed suicide by stepping in front of a tractor trailer on a highway near her home. I read her suicide note online the next day. I am just three months older than her.

The Pink Triangle was the arm band used to designate prisoners charged with homosexuality in Nazi concentration camps. It has been used since the 1980s as a symbol of queer resistance, especially in the face of the AIDS crisis.

p. 63 | Penelope / Odysseus

Remember Odysseus, of Trojan War fame, referenced in "Odysseus Leaving Aeaea"? Well, while he spends ten years fighting in the Trojan War and then ten more years trying to get home to Ithaca, there is a woman waiting for him. That woman is named Penelope, and she spends twenty years raising their son, Telemachus, and warding off a horde of suitors, who believe Odysseus is dead and want her to remarry.

She uses a number of guises to avoid remarrying and she is quite successful. She and her husband are reunited, and she is often upheld as a paradigm of marital faithfulness.

The line "one must imagine // Penelope happy" is a play on Albert Camus' essay "The Myth of Sisyphus," which ends with the sentence "One must imagine Sisyphus happy." Sisyphus is a mythical figure cursed to roll a giant stone up a hill in Hades, only for the stone to roll back down the hill when he's finished, over and over again for eternity.

p. 64 | Bacchus, Bronx

Bacchus is the sometimes-Greek and most-of-the-time-Roman name for Dionysus. He is the god of wine, insanity, fruit, fertility, and theater – so, a queer. His cult members are known for their extreme acts of violence while caught up in ritual frenzy – see Euripides' *The Bacchae* and Donna Tart's *The Secret History*.

pp. 65-66 | Hyacinthus / Apollo

Apollo is one of the Olympic deities that wears a lot of hats – he's the god of archery, music, prophecy, medicine, and the sun, among other things. Apollo has many lovers, many of them mortal men, and one of those mortal men is a Spartan athlete, Hyacinthus. One day, Apollo and Hyacinthus are tossing the discus back and forth, and Zephyrus, one of the wind gods, is jealous. Zephyrus blows the discus into a direct collision course with Hyacinthus' skull, killing him. Apollo is supposed to have created the flower, hyacinth, out of Hyacinthus' blood.

p. 67 | Astraeus / Eos

Eos, goddess and personification of the dawn, and her husband, Astraeus, a second-generation Titan (don't worry about it) associated with stars, are a minor-deity power couple. There's not actually that much else about their story that inspired this poem, though they are notably the parents of the Anemoi, the Four Winds.

p. 68 | Muse Prayer

"The Muse" has become a general term for the inspirational force behind all art, but in ancient Greek myth they are a specific group of goddesses, usually nine, named Calliope, Clio, Polyhymnia, Euterpe, Terpsichore, Erato, Melpomene, Thalia, and Urania.

The epigram is a quote from "The Writing Life" in Alexander Chee's book *How to Write an Autobiographical Novel*.

pp. 72-83 | The Caeneid

Caenis, daughter of Elatus, King of the Lapiths, is born in Thessaly. When she's a young woman, Poseidon rapes her and, as consolation, offers her anything she asks for. She asks to be made a man in hopes it will protect her from future assault. Poseidon grants her request and throws in impenetrable skin to sweeten the deal. Caeneus, as he comes to be called, becomes King of the Lapiths in turn.

Caeneus leads his men into the Centauromachy, the war between the Lapiths and the centaurs. The centaur Latreus mocks him in a speech that's pretty standard material for transphobes to this day, if a little more eloquent than your average Twitter user. When the centaurs capture him, they know his skin can't be broken by any weapon, so they bury him under stones until he is crushed to death inside his own body (which could mean nothing). In Ovid's version of the story, Caeneus is transformed into a yellow bird that rises out of his funeral pyre.

The People's Beach at Jacob Riis Park, referenced in "Caeneus / Poseidon," is a beach in Brooklyn popular among queer people.

The opening line of the poem "Caeneus' Metamorphosis," "Retired from slut – new career / in sad," references Mitski's 2013 album, "Retired from Sad, New Career in Business."

BIBLIOGRAPHY

Camus, Albert. *The Myth of Sisyphus and Other Essays*. Vintage, 2018.

Carson, Anne. *Eros the Bittersweet: An Essay*. Princeton University Press, 2023.

D'Aulaire, Ingri, and Edgar Parin D'Aulaire. *D'Aulaires' Book of Greek Myths*. Delacorte Press, 1992.

Haynes, Natalie. *Divine Might: Goddesses in Greek Myth*. Pan Macmillan, 2023.

-----. *Pandora's Jar: Women in the Greek Myths*. Pan Macmillan, 2020.

Highwater, Hellen. "Art by H. Highwater." *Highwater Studio*, 2024, www.highwater-studio.com/.

Homer. *The Iliad*. Edited by Bernard Knox. Translated by Robert Fagles, Penguin Classics, 1998.

-----. *The Iliad*. Translated by Emily R. Wilson, W.W. Norton & Company, 2024.

-----. *The Odyssey*. Edited by Bernard Knox. Translated by Robert Fagles, Penguin Classics, 1999.

-----. *The Odyssey*. Translated by Emily R. Wilson, W.W. Norton & Company, 2018.

Moonface. "This One's for the Dancer & This One's for the Dancer's Bouquet." Spencer Krug, Toronto.

Morales, Helen. *Antigone Rising: the Subversive Power of the Ancient Myths*. Bold Type Books, 2020.

Ovid. *Metamorphoses*. Translated by Stephanie McCarter, Penguin Classics, 2022.

-----. *The Metamorphoses*. Translated by Frank Justus Miller, Barnes & Noble Classics, 2005.

Reynolds, Margaret. *The Sappho Companion*. Palgrave, 2001.

Sappho. *If Not, Winter: Fragments of Sappho*. Translated by Anne Carson, Vintage, 2003.

-----. *Sappho*. Translated by Mary Barnard, University of California Press, 2012.

Smith, William. "COMA, the Hair." *Greek and Roman Hairstyles (Smith's Dictionary, 1875)*, University of Chicago, 18 Apr. 2018, penelope.uchicago.edu/Thayer/E/Roman/Texts/secondary/SMIGRA*/Coma.html.

ACKNOWLEDGEMENTS

A great many people contributed to the writing of this book over the seven years since I wrote the first Caeneus poem, and there were many before that who helped shape me as a writer. It's quite likely many of them I'll forget to mention. If I have left you off of this list, I owe you a meal – call any time to cash in. In no particular order, I'd like to thank:

The lovers and friends, past and present, who inspired many of these poems; Alex McParland, a writer, artist, and friend without whom my life would be less than it is; Sandra Goldstein Lehnert, whose scholarship and friendship have shaped me since we met; Aggie Johnson, for their friendship and for creating the beautiful cover art for this book; Belinda Farley, whose poetic spirit never fails to inspire me; Brian Cordell and James Hoch, whose advice I didn't always take but who gave the tools I needed; the fellow poets in writing workshops at Bergen Community College and Ramapo College of New Jersey who helped me shape my voice; Tom, Tina, and Maggie, the family I was born into; Azarel, Olive, Jamie, Amal, Sam, Maeve, Everett, Lily, Joon, and everyone else who makes up the family I've made.

PUBLICATIONS

The following publications were the original home to earlier versions of poems in this collection:

Eunoia Review: 'Astraeus / Eos,' 'Athenian Ritual,' 'Caeneus Redux,' 'Caenis in Thessaly,' 'Ganymede / Zeus,' 'Hyacinthus / Apollo'

Neologism Poetry Journal: 'Persephone / Hades'

Querencia Quarterly: 'Labors of Heracles'

Union Spring Literary Review: 'The Other Sappho'

ABOUT BIRCH

Birch Wiley (they/them) is a transsexual poet living in New York. Their work can be found in *Pleiades*, *Voicemail Poems*, and *Querencia Quarterly*, among others. *Mythweaver* is their first book. You can learn more about them at birchwiley.com.

ABOUT nw{p}

new words {press} is a non-profit poetry press publishing trans* & gender-expansive poets & hybrid writers.

support our efforts & the incredible writers we publish. visit us at **newwordspress.com**